This book belongs to

_____

This book is dedicated to my children - Mikey, Kobe, and Jojo.
It is more blessed to give than to receive.

# Money Ninja

By Mary Nhin

Pictures by
Jelena Stupar

Money Ninja was filling his candy machine and collecting the money he made.

Meanwhile, Unplugged Ninja was explaining what he was going to do with his birthday money. "After I buy 5 packs of Pokemon cards, I'm going to buy a new remote control for my PC."

That's awesome!

After they got home, Money Ninja sold lemonade while Unplugged Ninja continued to talk about spending his money.

After an afternoon of selling lemonade, Money Ninja decided to make a video for his YouTube Channel. He had been documenting the entire day.

He was making money from his YouTube channel, just sharing his daily happenings.

When they arrived at room #4322, Money Ninja handed his hard-earned money to Brave Ninja's mother.

Brave Ninja had recently been diagnosed with Leukemia.
The money was going to help pay his doctor bills.

On the way home, Money Ninja explained, "You can do other things with your money besides spend it, you know? You can invest it, save it, or donate it."

"I've never thought about that," said Unplugged Ninja.

"When I got money for my birthday, one of the first things I did was to save some for my car. By the time I turn 16, I'll have $10,000 saved up in my bank account," explained Money Ninja.

Saving helps us develop delayed gratification. That's a good quality to have. It means we're patient.

## Money Ninja Tip

If you deposit $100 into a checking account, your money will collect interest. The bank may pay you up to $3. So, you can turn $100 into $103.

"Another thing I did with my birthday money was invest it. I invested in a lemonade stand, candy machines, and equipment for a YouTube channel," continued Money Ninja.

Investing helps us to become money-savvy, which means smart with money.

$10 → $20

 Money Ninja Tip

If you invest $10 into your business, like the lemonade stand, and you make $20 back, you just doubled your money.

"Finally, the last thing I did with my birthday money was donate it. Donating to my church and to those in need makes me feel happy."

**Money Ninja Tip**

Sometimes what you do with your money gives you things you can't see but that you can feel.

Developing delayed gratification, money-savvy skills, and donating to those in need are a ninja's best weapons against instant gratification and greed.

Sign up for new Ninja book releases at
GrowGrit.co

Made in the USA
Coppell, TX
22 May 2020

26281143R00017